WHAT ON EARTH IS A
GUANACO

?

EDWARD R. RICCIUTI

A BLACKBIRCH PRESS BOOK
WOODBRIDGE, CONNECTICUT

Published by Blackbirch Press, Inc.
One Bradley Road, Suite 104
Woodbridge, CT 06525

©1994 Blackbirch Press, Inc.
First Edition

Printed in Hong Kong

10 9 8 7 6 5 4 3 2 1

Photo Credits

Cover, title page: ©Barbara J. Wright/Animals Animals.
Page 5: ©F. Gohier/Photo Researchers, Inc; pages 6—7: ©Mike Jackson/Photo Researchers, Inc.; page 8: ©Margot Conte/Animals Animals; page11: ©Miriam Austerman/ Animals Animals; page13: ©Mark Newman/Photo Researchers, Inc; pages 14—15: ©E.R. Degginger/Animals Animals; page16: ©Joe McDonald/Animals Animals; page17: ©Don Enger/Animals Animals; pages 18—19: ©Joe McDonald/Animals Animals; page 21: ©Robert W. Hernandez/Photo Researchers, Inc; pages 22—23: ©Mike Jackson/Photo Researchers, Inc; page 25: ©Susan Jones/Animals Animals; page 26: ©Margot Conte/Animals Animals; page 27: ©Mark Newman/Photo Researchers, Inc; pages 28—29: ©F. Gohier/Photo Researchers, Inc; page 30: ©Mark Newman/Photo Researchers, Inc.
Map on page 12 by Blackbirch Press, Inc.

Library of Congress Cataloging-in-Publication Data
Ricciuti, Edward R.
What on earth is a guanaco? / Edward R. Ricciuti. — 1st ed.
    p.   cm. — (What on earth series)
    Includes bibliographical references (p.   ) and index.
    ISBN 1-56711-095-9 : $12.95
    1. Guanaco—Juvenile literature.   [1. Guanaco.   2. Llama. (Genus)]
I. Title. II. Series.
QL737.U54R53   1994
599.73'6—dc20   94-22523
                                                                CIP
                                                                 AC

What does it look like?

Where does it live?

What does it eat?

How does it reproduce?

How does it survive?

TURN THESE PAGES AND FIND OUT!

A guanaco is a large animal that looks a lot like a llama or a camel. It has a long, slender neck and a slender snout. It also has a small head and long legs. Most of its body is covered in soft wool. Like camels and llamas, guanacos have large eyes with thick eyelashes. Their large eyes provide them with excellent vision and allow them to see great distances.

GUANACOS ARE LARGE
BUT DELICATE-LOOKING
ANIMALS, WITH LONG
NECKS AND SLENDER LEGS.

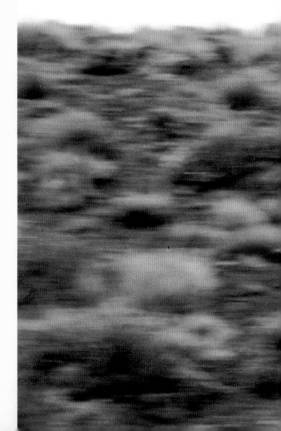

The guanaco is a member of an animal group called "camelids." There are five other species in this group. They are the llama, alpaca, vicuña, Bactrian camel, and dromedary. Most people are familiar with the Bactrian camel and the dromedary. The Bactrian is the camel with two humps, the dromedary has only one.

Camelid feet have two toes, each with a hard nail at the tip and a thick, moveable pad underneath. The knees of camelids are on the lower part of their legs. When a camelid runs, the rear leg and front leg on the same side of the body move at the same time.

WITH THEIR LONG LEGS, GUANACOS ARE BOTH SPEEDY AND GRACEFUL.

The scientific name of the guanaco is *Llama guanicoe*. The name comes from words used by ancient people in South America who described this animal. South America is the home of the guanaco, as well as the vicuña, llama, and alpaca. The guanaco and vicuña are wild. The llama and alpaca are domestic, or raised by people.

Most guanacos stand about 4 feet (1 meter) high at the shoulders. They usually weigh between 200 pounds (90 kilograms) and 260 pounds (118 kilograms). Most of a guanaco's body is covered by wool that is dark brown on its back and sides, and white underneath. Its face is almost all black.

When an adult guanaco wants to lie down, it bends its front knees until they touch the ground. Next, it lowers its hindquarters and then its chest to the ground. Guanacos sit with their legs under their bodies.

The long legs of guanacos help them cover ground quickly. They can run at a speed of more than 30 miles (48 kilometers) an hour. They can also swim.

IN ORDER TO SIT, GUANACOS MUST BEND THEIR KNEES UNTIL THEY TOUCH THE GROUND.

Guanacos are found in South America. They roam the nations of Peru, Chile, Bolivia and, most of all, Argentina. They live in open country, from the lowlands up to 14,000 feet (4,270 meters) high—way up in the Andes mountains. At that height, the air can be bitterly cold. But low temperatures do not bother guanacos. Neither does heat, unless the climate is moist. Their thick, wooly coats insulate them and protect them from the extreme temperatures.

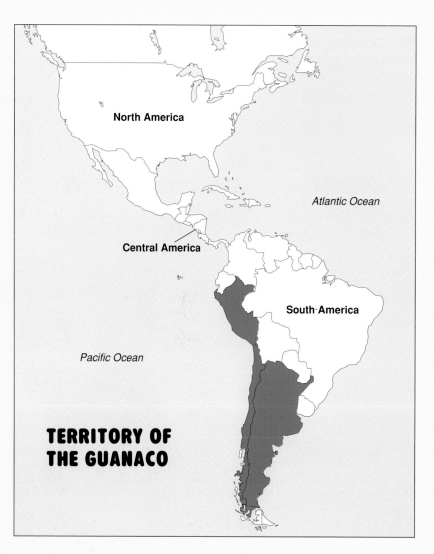

North America

Atlantic Ocean

Central America

South America

Pacific Ocean

**TERRITORY OF
THE GUANACO**

GUANACOS ARE FOUND
IN SOUTH AMERICA AND
OFTEN LIVE AROUND
MOUNTAINS, AT HIGH
ALTITUDES.

The guanaco can survive in dry places, even desert, because its body uses very little water. It can survive for long periods simply on the moisture in the plants that it eats.

Because guanacos live in areas that get very little rainfall, few trees grow in their habitat. Most plants that grow in the guanaco's surroundings are tough grasses and shrubs. Guanacos feed largely on these grasses and on the leaves of shrubs. The guanaco's broad front teeth enable it to nip off and chew pieces of these plants, even though they are quite tough.

BECAUSE THEIR HABITAT CONTAINS FEW PLANTS, GUANACOS MUST SURVIVE BY EATING MOSTLY SHRUBS AND GRASSES.

Few animals attack and eat guanacos. Andean condors, which are a kind of vulture, may attack a very young guanaco, especially if the youngster is weak or sick. Mountain lions may hunt guanacos if their usual food is scarce, but this is not very common. For the most part, guanacos live peacefully in their surroundings and are not bothered by other animals.

16

MOUNTAIN LIONS SHARE THE GUANACO'S HABITAT.

any other interesting animals inhabit the plains and mountains of guanaco and vicuña country. The most spectacular of them is the Andean condor, with wings more than 10 feet (3 meters) across. Lakes on plateaus high in the Andes are home to two kinds of flamingos, which gather in great flocks to feed. On the lowland plains, another large bird, the rhea, is a neighbor

A SMALL HERD OF GUANACOS GRAZES ON THE FLAT, OPEN PLAINS OF ARGENTINA.

of guanacos. The rhea resembles an ostrich. Rheas are 5 feet (2 meters) tall and cannot fly. Certain mammals share guanaco country as well. They include a small deer called the guemal, rodents such as chinchillas and the rat-like tuco-tuco, and mountain lions. In some areas, guanacos wander close to ocean beaches, where penguins and sea lions reside.

Guanacos escape from danger by running. When it is angry or frightened, a male guanaco will scream loudly, alerting all others who can hear it. Guanacos sometimes run for high ground in order to seek protection. On higher ground, they can more easily see any possible danger.

GUANACOS RELY ON THEIR EYESIGHT AND SPEED TO PROTECT THEM FROM POSSIBLE ENEMIES.

A guanaco family group usually has about 16 members. Each family is headed by an adult male. The rest of the group is made up of females and young up to 15 months old. The family usually feeds within an area, or territory, of about 60 acres (24 hectares). The head of a guanaco family will fight to keep other males away from his females. When two males fight, each tries to push

**A GUANACO FAMILY GROUP IS HEADED BY
AN ADULT MALE.**

the other down to its knees. During a fight, they
often kick, bang chests, and snap at each other's
legs. With long necks crossed, they push and
shove until one male quits or goes down.

   An angry guanaco may also spit saliva and
stomach juice at an enemy. Sometimes males spit
at each other during fights. A male may also spit
at a female who does not want to mate with him.

A female guanaco mates every other year, in August or September. When mating, the female lies down while the male stands over her. When they mate, the male's sex cells, or sperm, enter the female. Inside the female, a sperm joins her egg in a process called fertilization.

Once an egg is fertilized, a new offspring begins to develop. The female gives birth to a single baby about a year after mating. Newborn guanacos vary in weight, from 12 pounds (5 kilograms) to 30 pounds (14 kilograms). Though their muscles are still new, baby guanacos can jump and run almost as soon as they are born!

A FEMALE GUANACO LIES DOWN IN PREPARATION FOR GIVING BIRTH.

A YOUNG GUANACO, ONLY A FEW MONTHS OLD.

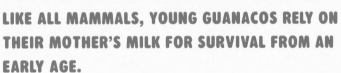

LIKE ALL MAMMALS, YOUNG GUANACOS RELY ON THEIR MOTHER'S MILK FOR SURVIVAL FROM AN EARLY AGE.

Young guanacos live on their mother's milk for about three months. Then they start to eat plants. When they are between 13 and 15 months old, the head male in the family chases them away.

Once on their own, young females eventually join the families of other adult males. The young males gather in groups and stay together for three to four years. After that, the groups break up as the males try to gather families of their own.

GUANACO POPULATIONS HAVE DECREASED
A GREAT DEAL IN RECENT YEARS.

There are about half a million guanacos in the wild. This may sound like a large number but it is not. Guanacos have disappeared from many places in which they once lived. They have been killed for their valuable hides and for their meat. Guanacos have also been killed by ranchers, who want to keep precious grass for their sheep. Laws now control or completely ban guanaco hunting. But many animals are still killed illegally.

IN ORDER TO SURVIVE, GUANACOS MUST BE PROTECTED BY LAWS THAT PREVENT ILLEGAL HUNTING AND CAPTURING.

Most people who live near guanacos are very poor. They are often tempted to get money from the sale of guanaco hides, wool, and meat. Conservationists are seeking ways for people to use guanacos without killing them. One way is to round guanacos up, clip their wool, and then release them. Another is to allow hunting of guanacos where they are numerous. This must be carefully watched to make sure that enough young replace those that are killed. Where guanacos are scarce, they must remain protected from people who try to hunt them illegally.

Glossary

camelids The name for all members of the camel family.

egg Female sex cell.

fertilization The union of sperm and egg that creates a new organism.

habitat Surroundings that provide an animal with space, shelter, and food.

insulate Protect from extreme temperatures.

mammal A group of animals, including humans, that produce their own body heat, have hair, and feed their young on milk.

sperm Male sex cell.

Further Reading

Arnold, Caroline. *Camel.* New York: Morrow Junior Books, 1992.

Cobb, Vicki. *This Place Is High.* New York: Walker and Co., 1989.

Fagan, Elizabeth G. *Rand McNally Children's Atlas of World Wildlife.* Chicago: Rand McNally, 1993.

Jones, Susan L. *Llamas: Wooly, Winsome, and Wonderful.* Scottsdale, AZ: 1987.

LaBonte, Gail. *The Llama.* New York: Dillon, 1988.

Morrison, Marion. *Ecuador, Peru, Bolivia.* Morristown, NJ: Raintree Steck-Vaughn, 1992.

32

What On Earth
Is a Guanaco?

Index